Thame to Watlington

IN OLD PHOTOGRAPHS

Couching Street, Watlington, *c.* 1910, is a mixture of seventeenth to nineteenth-century buildings characteristic of small market towns. The view looks from the Brook Street end towards the High Street and Town Hall. Searley's shop is the building at the far end of the street. Bowler's Piece and the Red Lion are in the foreground, right.

Thame to Watlington

IN OLD PHOTOGRAPHS

Compiled by NANCY HOOD

Alan Sutton Publishing Limited
Phoenix Mill · Far Thrupp
Stroud · Gloucestershire

OXFORDSHIRE BOOKS

First published 1993

Cover illustration: Market day for sheep in the Cornmarket, Thame, *c.* 1900. Sheep were brought to market in carts, the hurdles providing both cover during transport and the pens at market. The livestock markets were often a source of disease and they were closed on several occasions in the nineteenth century. In 1951 the cattle market was moved to a site off the main street, on North Street.

British Library Cataloguing
in Publication Data

Hood, Nancy
   Thame to Watlington in Old Photographs
   I. Title
   942.57

ISBN 0-7509-0521-2

Typeset in 9/10 Sabon.
Typesetting and origination by
Alan Sutton Publishing Limited.
Printed in Great Britain by
Redwood Books, Trowbridge, Wiltshire.

Newington, a hamlet with a manor house and a church, *c.* 1920.

Contents

Chinnor station in 1919. The village was served by this little halt on the Watlington branch line until 1957.

Introduction

A slow, almost imperceptible climb up the Chilterns from east to west along the motorway ends at the escarpment, with a panoramic view over all Oxfordshire: Berkshire Downs to the south, Cotswolds (on a clear day) on the western skyline, and clay vale straight ahead. The area covered by the photographs in this book lies between the Chiltern scarp and the small ridge of limestone which prevents a view of Oxford. The landscape looks deceptively flat from here; a journey off the M40 winds through tiny valleys in the lower chalk and greensand belts at·the foot of the scarp, and follows gentle ridges of gravel above the Gault clay vale with its numerous brooks. These rise from springs at the foot of the scarp, flow into the River Thame, and then into the Thames proper at Dorchester. The villages are tucked away in sheltered dips; the major landmarks are the fairly recent cooling towers of Didcot power station to the south and the chimney stacks of Chinnor cement works a little to the north.

Up on the Chiltern ridge, the Nature Reserve of Aston Rowant offers a variety of plant life, from woodland to the open juniper, gorse and broom scrub and grassland characteristic of the chalk and clay-with-flints soils.

Woodland flowers and shrubs – bluebells, primroses, wood anemones, violets, as well as hawthorns and brambles – are to be found in the woods and hedges, with herbs and orchids in the open grassland. The wild raspberry can still be found in the Chilterns.

Some of the hedges are a thousand years old, from the time of the Saxon colonization of the area, and the present-day parishes reflect these ancient divisions in their topography. Along the Chiltern scarp the villages lie at the valley's edge, watered by brooks from the springs which occur periodically along the scarp foot. Arable fields cluster around each village, and up the slope the fields give way to scrub, woodland and upland pasture, all pieces of the jigsaw of the village economy. The boundaries stretch up the hill either side of the settlement, forming long, narrow, strip parishes. From Chinnor in the north-east to Watlington, the settlements of Crowell, Kingston Blount, Aston Rowant, Lewknor and Pyrton follow the spring line and are connected by the Lower Icknield Way. Lewknor, Pyrton, Binfield, Langtree and Ewelme preserve the Anglo-Saxon grouping of the four and a half hundreds, known as the Chiltern Hundreds, part of the manor of Benson. As early as the sixth or seventh century the area was known as 'Cilternsaetna', the land of Chiltern dwellers.

The topography of the Chilterns is reflected in the place names given by the Anglo-Saxons: Chinnor, Stonor and Lewknor are named after the 'ora' or elongated hill, whereas a 'dun' is a rounded hill, as in Assendon, and a 'hoh' is a shoulder of a ridge which stands out at an angle, as in Ivinghoe. The Hampdens, Missendens and Hambleden are on the long, gently rising valleys of the dip-slope of the hills, the 'dens' and the 'cumbs' are at the heads of the valleys, as in Swyncombe and Wycombe. Ewelme, Crowell and Britwell take their names from the springs or 'wells'.

Above the villages, the Upper Icknield Way, a ridgeway along the Chilterns, was the dry winter route, part of the trade and droveway system from prehistoric times. Dr Plot in the *Natural History of Oxfordshire* (1677) describes its reputation: 'it passes through no Town or Village in the County, but only Goreing; nor does it (as I hear) scarce anywhere else, for which Reason 'tis much used by stealers of Cattle'.

One threat to successful settlement in the hills was the local climate which was associated with the steep scarp facing the vale. This was described by Arthur Young in the report on Oxfordshire to the Board of Agriculture in 1813: 'It is cold, also, upon and near the Chiltern hills, especially on the poor white lands at the foot of the hills; where it is always to be observed, that the frost will take effect sooner, and continue longer on that soil, than it does on the deeper lands further situated from the hills. The climate of the Chiltern country is moist, on account of the fogs, which are more frequent on the hills and woods than in the Vale.' However, he observed that the clay-with-flints could produce some of the best soils in the county, and so it was worthwhile to clear the land. He observed that the aspect of the Chilterns appeared 'a great range of beechwoods, intermixed with chalk and flint fields'. The chalk itself was a handy source of lime and added fertility to the fields, which had the problem of thin topsoil. 'Chalk makes a rich Father but a poor Son', and

7

gradually rye and grasses for fodder replaced wheat on the upland fields, noted Dr Plot. At Britwell and Watlington he saw rags and taylors' shreds used for manure – the shreds contained the salts of the fullers' earth used in their preparation, but the worn rags were thought to be better as they were 'very well sated with urinous salts, contracted from the Sweat and continual Perspiration attending their bodies'.

The mixed farming – fields, woodland, with plenty of upland pasture and grazing – allowed a self-sufficiency to develop in the Chiltern parishes, which was already evident in the numbers of freeholders returned in the Domesday survey of 1086. Nineteen of the twenty-three freeholders in the county were in the Chilterns. Population growth in the early Middle Ages accounted for a number of smaller settlements attached to assarts, or clearings, up in the hills – one such settlement was excavated at Sadler's Wood, above Lewknor, during the building of the M40. Spriggs Holly is a daughter settlement above Chinnor, and Christmas Common above Watlington. Some of the boundary ditches between the field closes and the woods, known as 'woodbanks', can be seen in woodland today.

A contrasting pattern developed in the vale parishes, where open fields persisted until the nineteenth century. 'Descending the Chiltern Hills, from Stokenchurch to Tetsworth, the vale is open field, and the soil exceedingly good; a brown strong loam on a moist bottom, yields great crops of wheat' reported Arthur Young, but as an exponent of the enclosure of open fields in the name of progress, he despaired of the attitude of the local farmers. Opposition to enclosure stemmed from 'ignorance, bigotry, and self interestedness, of the several occupiers . . . fearful of deviating from the old beaten track . . . others of a sour morose temper, who think all old ways best . . . of an envious jealous disposition, who will not agree to any alterations; here 'the Goths and Vandals of open fields touch the civilisation of enclosures'. Young had praise for Stadhampton: 'Good arable, enclosed, convertible, some meadow', but scorn for Chalgrove: 'Clay; sad roads, and bad husbandry: all open'.

The dairy farming was praised, however, especially around Waterperry, Waterstock, Aldbury, Tiddington and Chiselhampton, where usually Shorthorn cows were kept. Once there were rail connections to London, milk could be sent in bulk to market.

The vale parishes suffered greatly in the agricultural depressions of the nineteenth century, and poverty among the agricultural labourers was severe enough to encourage assisted emigration to Australia for some families in the 1840s. Women contributed to the family earnings through outwork, usually lacemaking and straw-plaiting at home. Lace schools at Chinnor and Aston Rowant kept young girls working eleven hours a day, and of the 286 lacemakers in the village in 1851, 86 were children. The craft enjoyed a revival after the 1851 Great Exhibition, as did chair-making, but pillow-lace had been supplanted by machine-made or foreign lace by the end of the century.

In the Chilterns, where chair-making was developing in the beech woods, women could work at the caning of the chair seats, while men worked at bodging and turning chair legs in the woods, or assembling chairs in barns and cottage workshops. Chinnor had forty-three chairmakers in 1851. Chair-making was divided into a number of separate processes and skills, which could be carried out locally until mechanization firmly rooted it in the factories of High Wycombe, and imported timber competed with home-grown beech.

Other sidelines included the growing and gathering of watercress along the brooks, a local industry which lasted until recently at Ewelme. After 1872 cress could be sent to London quickly by train, and villages such as Chinnor and Lewknor along the Watlington line benefited from this connection. In addition to cress at Chinnor, ducks were farmed and sent to London. There has also been a tradition of honey production at Ewelme.

Stone quarries, masonry and ironworks were additional prospects for skilled work in Great and Little Haseley, and these were relatively prosperous villages. Thame had a brick and tile works, but lack of a reliable water supply prevented brewing from becoming a major local industry there. At Watlington, however, the local brewery on Brook Street lasted until the First World War.

Thame and Watlington are the two market towns in the area, and have been since the Middle Ages. Watlington's Wednesday market was established by charter in 1252. In 1665 a novel brick market house and Town Hall replaced the earlier one, at the major crossroads of the town. Soon, grand new houses, or the re-fronting of older cottages, in red and blue brick lined the streets leading to it, moving the focus of the town away from the church.

The centre of Thame also shifted from the manor at Priest End near the church, with the grant of a market by the Bishop of Lincoln and the layout of a new planned town in 1221–7. A long, wide market place was set out and lined with shops backed by narrow burgage plots. By 1305 seventy-six were taken up, and Thame soon had a population of over one thousand. Although shops and houses have encroached on the market place in the middle of the High Street, dividing it into upper and lower halves, the original plan is still apparent. A market was held on separate days for cattle, sheep, pigs and dairy cows.

'I remember the roads of Oxfordshire forty years ago, when they were in a condition formidable to the bones of all who travelled on wheels', was Arthur Young's comment on the improvements brought about by the turnpiking of the main routes. The importance of the route from London through High Wycombe to Oxford (later the A40) ensured that this road was turnpiked early, by 1718. Stagecoach journeys, which took two days in the seventeenth century, could be made in a day by 1800. Six-horse wagons were used up Aston Hill. Heavy freight, however, continued to go to London by barge from Henley down the Thames, and wood, barley for malting, and corn were taken to Henley to market.

The Oxford Canal to Coventry opened in 1790, and the Grand Union Canal between the Midlands and London reached Tring in 1799; branches opened to Wendover and Aylesbury, and the price of coal in the area was cut by half. At this time many of the local watermills were converted to steam power.

A railway line through the Chilterns, from London to Oxford or to

Birmingham, was unattractive financially; a plan to run a line through the Wendover Gap was defeated by a combination of the large landowners, the Turnpike Trusts, the Canal Company and the coach and wagon proprietors. Many other schemes were successfully resisted for a number of years by local landowners. When finally built, the main lines ran north, via Aylesbury, or south, along the Thames corridor. The Chilterns and the vale were served by branch lines from the Great Western Railway: 1854–62, High Wycombe to Princes Risborough, and 1864, Princes Risborough to Thame and Oxford. Other branches connected Princes Risborough to Aylesbury in 1863, and to Watlington in 1872. In this century these lines have proved most vulnerable to competition from freight carriers by road, and many were closed in the 1950s and 1960s.

With the building of the M40 in 1972/3, the area has been opened up to much quicker road access to and from London. With this convenience have come the pressures for development, for industry and housing within reach of London; for recreational and leisure use of the Chilterns and 'set aside' farmland. Planning constraints and local resistance have defeated the proposed new town of 'Stone Bassett' near the M40 at Great Milton, and limited industrial estates to the edges of Oxford and Banbury.

The Chilterns were made an Area of Outstanding Natural Beauty in 1964, and the decision soon after to route the M40 through the Aston Rowant Nature Reserve provoked nationwide controversy. The counties of Hertfordshire, Bedfordshire, Buckinghamshire and Oxfordshire, and the twelve district authorities, now co-operate on the management of the woods and the public use of the 309 square miles of landscape for recreation. Away from the motorway, quiet places are still to be found, much as they appear in the photographs in this book.

Nancy Hood
August 1993

Market Towns: Thame

The new Town Hall, 1888, stands at the heart of Thame, where the exceptionally wide Upper and Lower High Streets are interrupted by the markets, Cornmarket and Buttermarket. Pevsner's *Buildings of England* calls it a feeble Jacobean design, and Thame certainly has many more elegant buildings dating from a hundred years earlier. Upkeep has proved too much for the Town Council, and the cellar has been abandoned to the damp.

St Mary's church from the Aylesbury Road, 1884. The thirteenth-century church was enlarged in the fourteenth and fifteenth centuries in keeping with the prosperity of the market town. Inside are some very fine brasses of the Quatremains and the Dormers, and the grand, Flemish-style tomb of Lord Williams and his wife Elizabeth (1559).

Priest End, c. 1910. This part of Thame around the church is the area of early settlement, before the founding to the east of the new town and market place in the thirteenth century. Recent excavations during works in the church have uncovered burials which pre-date the present building.

Free School and almshouses, *c.* 1887. Thame's major benefactor was Lord Williams (1500–59), who served at court in many capacities and was able to benefit personally from the sale of the monastic properties in the 1530s. He bought up the lands of Thame Abbey, and left endowments in his will to found a 'Free School' and almshouses. The school, seen in the background here when it had already moved to new premises on the Oxford Road, kept forty to fifty pupils and two teachers. The almshouses, on the left, kept five old men and one old woman.

The house, formerly the Greyhound Inn, where John Hampden died in 1643, having been mortally wounded at the Battle of Chalgrove during the Civil War. He was from Thame, educated at Lord Williams' School, and led the local opposition to the Ship Money tax of Charles I. The area was sympathetic to the Parliamentarians and consequently suffered at the hands of the Royalists from time to time. This house has suffered too: its later shop front alterations are pure vandalism; the arch now leads to the new car park and supermarket.

Lower High Street before 1887, looking at the old Town Hall. This side of the street is a line of almost unspoiled Georgian buildings – some are sixteenth to seventeenth century, re-fronted with brick in the Georgian style. At the back gables or half-timbering are often revealed.

High Street from the Town Hall, looking towards Lower High Street and Oxford Road, 1890. Handsome Georgian houses mix with smaller terraces and pubs. The local Georgian made much use of silver-blue and red chequerboard patterning, and some early cottages were simply stuccoed over.

Cornmarket and Upper High Street in the 1870s. There is little new building here.

Thame cattle market, Upper High Street, in the 1920s. The market place has been paved and posts provided for tethering the animals after the sanitary problems of the past. For sale here are shorthorns, the preferred type of cattle in the area.

Cornmarket, looking towards Upper High Street, was photographed by Henry Taunt of Oxford around 1900. A chemist has occupied the shop, right foreground, for nearly two centuries. Next to it was Loader and Son, the corn merchants, and beyond is the Spread Eagle Hotel, one of the finest frontages in Thame, dating from 1740. Some Victorian building has been fitted into this side of Cornmarket and Upper High Street: Lloyds Bank with its multi-coloured brickwork, arches and gables, and in the distance on the right the two stone chapels, first the Methodist of 1876, and further along, on Upper High Street, the Congregational chapel of 1871.

High Street and Middle Way, with Buttermarket leading off on the left, in 1904. These shops are long-standing encroachments on to the wide space allowed for the market in the original town layout, and preserve a medieval flavour in their haphazard arrangement. The buildings date from the sixteenth and seventeenth centuries.

Nos 81–89 High Street from a postcard of 1907. The cottage on the right has been remodelled several times.

Upper High Street, looking towards the centre, 1910. The cattle and sheep markets fill the wide street on market days, and almost every other house is a hotel or pub. Thame had over thirty at this time. Whitehound pond on the left was of little use – it was so stagnant that horses refused to drink from it. It was cleaned up finally when the war memorial was built in 1921.

Upper High Street, looking towards Chinnor Road, c. 1880. On the left is the Swan Hotel, one of Thame's deceptive Georgian buildings – it dates from the sixteenth century, but was remodelled in the eighteenth, and its earlier details can be seen round the back. The street abounds with sixteenth-century gables and pretty red and blue brickwork; on the right is the newly built Congregational chapel.

The north side of the High Street, showing the bend into Lower High Street, *c.* 1910. No. 91, the large Georgian house on the right, was the Thame Literary Institute, which had moved in 1910 from its former premises in the market place. Appropriately, the house is now being considered as the home for a new, larger, library for Thame.

Lower High Street in the 1930s, looking towards the town centre, with the ominous presence of the motor car. Some of the early half-timbered buildings are visible – the thatched cottage on the right dates from the sixteenth century, as does the cottage facing down the street on the corner of Bell Lane. The first building on the left was a forge, and the tea shop next door is now a private house.

Chinnor Road from the town in 1910, looking east towards Chinnor and the Chilterns.

East Street, *c.* 1905, looking along the road to Princes Risborough. On the right is The Cross Keys, still a pub today, and the little terrace is an example of town expansion in the 1880s. The Cottage Hospital, built in 1898, is in the distance.

The Oxford Road entrance to the town, *c.* 1880. The two polygonal brick lodges on the left mark the entrance to Rycotewood Agricultural College, established in the former workhouse which dates from 1836/7. The Thame Union covered thirty-five parishes and could accommodate 350 men and women in the workhouse. In 1847, 2,790 vagrants passed through.

The China Shop on the corner of North Street and High Street, 1953–63. It was followed by Smith, Sons & Daughters and sold antiques, junk, and just about anything – a real landmark for local bargain hunters.

The Malt and Hops, Shirburn Street, Watlington, in the 1860s. James Lowe, the landlord, is standing outside with his wife Sarah. James, who was both a hairdresser and beer retailer, was born in 1818 and died in 1869; Sarah, born in 1822, was a Brant of Crowmarsh. Note Sarah's old-fashioned dress and hairstyle. The pub has since been demolished.

SECTION TWO

Market Towns: Watlington

The High Street and Town Hall under repair in 1907. Trindall's Garage is opposite the Town Hall, and Barclay's Bank occupies the site of the Three Crowns. In the foreground is Wilson's, a jeweller, and the entrance to the Lecture Hall is next door. The Lecture Hall was converted from a malthouse in 1858.

Watlington Town Hall and the corner of High Street, 1920. The Town Hall, the gift of Thomas Stonor in 1665, is a truly worthy brick building for a small market town and demonstrates the developing local skills in brickmaking. The arches are boastfully wide, and there is both moulded and toothed decoration. The market was held under the arches, and the rooms above were intended for a grammar school.

The High Street in the 1920s.

The High Street before the war memorial was built in The Cross on the right. The building facing is the Conservative and Unionist Club, with the chapel just visible at right angles to it on the right. The Royal Oak is in the background.

J. Trindall's first cycle shop on the High Street, 1902. Mr Trindall was a shoeing and general smith and cycle agent, and later also sold motorcycles.

Motorcyclists outside Trindall's shop in 1910. The shop, which had the first petrol pump in Watlington, had moved further towards the centre of town, in a building which was formerly The Crown.

Eli Smith's Brook Dairy, with daughters Dorie and Eva. The shop on the High Street is now the library.

Eli Smith and his son Bert in the yard behind the shop in the 1920s. The dairy was established in 1797; the cows were kept in West Meadow and were brought in every day for milking.

The Hare and Hounds on the High Street, a Georgian hotel of the usual red and blue brick.

Couching Street from a postcard dated 1906, with Old Bank House on the left. These buildings use the decorative blue and red brickwork to pleasing effect; Bank House is late Georgian, and the street has a number of earlier buildings. Richards Stores is on the right, but has been rebuilt.

Shirburn Street.

Munday's shop at The Cross, 1920s.

Glanville & Co.'s shop, decorated for Queen Victoria's Diamond Jubilee in 1897.

Watlington Brewery Company delivery wagon, 1910, behind the brewery on the corner of Brook Street and Couching Street. The houses in the background have since been demolished.

Frank Tappin's fourteen-seater charabanc outside Whitehorn Farm, Brook Street, in the 1920s. Frank and his wife are in the front, daughters Wyn and Olive in the back with the rest of the family. The charabanc took local groups on outings to the seaside, football and cricket matches. The signwriter inadvertently painted 'Tappings' and this was never changed.

Watlington Great Western Railway station at the turn of the century. The spur from the main Paddington–Birmingham line at Princes Risborough known as the Watlington branch, 8½ miles along the Chiltern escarpment foot, opened in 1872. Its passenger service operated until 1957, when many small branches closed as traffic turned to the roads.

The railway staff at Watlington station in 1924. Back row, left to right: Albert Brown (track), Darkie Sowden (track), Harry Humphries (driver), George Baker (porter), Harold 'Bumper' Jones (driver), Cecil Evetts (fireman), Peter Robinson (fireman), Tony Cliff (cleaner), Tommy Johnson (track). Front row: Charlie Hopkins (porter), Jimmy Nelms (guard), Mrs Siarey (clerk), Mr Pocock (stationmaster), Nobby Clarke, -?-, Harry Blackwell (track).

Brook Street from a postcard dated 1909. The brewery manager's house is on the corner of Couching Street (left), and the cottages on the further corner have since been demolished as far as Pilgrim Cottage.

The White Mark, Watlington, c. 1907. Children are picking blackberries at the foot of Hill Road, which climbs up through a much more open landscape on the scarp of the Chilterns than there is today. The hill is now wooded and looked after by the National Trust.

A view from The Green, Chalgrove, looking east down the High Street. The thatched cottages on the left are Laurel Farm and Granny's Cottage; the school yard is on the right. The cottage on the right has gone, and the lane leads off to the recreation ground.

SECTION THREE
Large Villages

The Green and war memorial, Chalgrove. A hedge now encloses the cottage gardens for privacy.

Chalgrove High Street, *c*. 1920, looking east with the corner of Coles Lane and Endways (sometimes known as Well House) on the left. On the right the barn has been replaced by a petrol station.

Chalgrove High Street, looking west with the bread delivery cart on the right.

CHALGROVE.

High Street, looking east with The Crown in the foreground.

On The Green outside The Crown public house, Chalgrove.

The brook, which runs the length of the High Street, from opposite The Green, looking towards the church. The cottages opposite are Charm Cottage and Granny's Cottage; beyond is the Red Lion.

Chalgrove High Street, showing more vanished cottages – those on the left were pulled down in the sixties.

High Street, *c.* 1904, looking west. Croxford's Stores is the handsome brick building on the right, next to the low building which was taken down two years later for the Village Hall. Further down the street is the large Old Rectory with its four dormer windows, now divided into separate dwellings. The farm in between is now Swinstead Court.

A view from The Green of the post office, High Street, Chalgrove, and Croxford's Stores (1869), looking west with the Rectory in the distance. There are modern houses infilling on the left.

The eastern approach to Chalgrove village at Church End. A housing estate lines the road to the right and the thatched Church Cottages on the left are now tiled.

High Street, looking east with Tudor Cottages on the right.

Chalgrove High Street with Woodbine Cottage in the distance, 1920s.

Another view of the High Street with Woodbine Cottage in the distance. The cottage was restored and tiled after a fire in 1982.

Chalgrove High Street, looking east. On the left is the White Hart, now a private house, and on the right is the Bakehouse, now demolished. Tudor Cottages are in the middle right.

High Street, looking east, showing Meadowview, behind which the new council estate has been built. These new housing estates built alongside the brook probably gave rise to the local saying that 'you don't belong to Chalgrove until you've fallen into it'.

High Street, Chalgrove, looking west with Endways on the right. The thatched barns on the left have been replaced by a petrol station. In the 1970s a custom developed of team races down the three-quarters-of-a-mile High Street, carrying a ball under and over each of the forty little arched bridges over the brook. The race ended at The Lamb.

High Street, looking east. The brook is a nineteenth-century diversion of the stream which was harnessed to drive the mill.

Cottage and brook, Chalgrove.

Lamb Corner, Chalgrove. This is now the entrance to the village from Oxford, but formerly the end of the village was a T-junction with Mill Lane, to the left, and Marley Lane. The cottage on the right is Jinnetts, *c.* 1690; The Lamb pub is out of the picture on the left, and the splendid tree has gone.

Mill Lane, Chalgrove, in the 1920s, looking towards Lamb Corner. The workshop on the left has since been demolished, but the peak of the roof of The Lamb can be seen behind, and the two last cottages of the High Street are in the background: Brook House was demolished in the sixties; Jinnetts Cottage is on the left. The owner of the dray must be in the pub!

Mill Lane. The forge is on the right, with a pile of stones for making up the road in the foreground. The Lamb is on the left.

Lamb Corner, Chalgrove. When the airfield was built in 1943, the road from Oxford was moved from the airfield site to join the High Street at its western end. The cottages are Jinnetts Cottage, Wishing Well Cottage, Brook House (now demolished), and April Cottage in the foreground.

Brook Cottage on the High Street, Chalgrove. This cottage features on its own on postcards and, with its pretty garden on the brook bank, is a chocolate-box scene. It now has two windows in the eaves. The neighbouring cottage is late nineteenth century.

High Street changes in 1963, viewed from the corner of Quartermain Road. New bungalows filled in spaces left by dilapidated workshops or old thatched cottages, in this case Poplar Farm.

Chinnor from the Chilterns

View of Chinnor in the 1920s from the Chilterns, looking north and west. The village was laid out on a large square; the cluster of houses on the right indicates the High Street, and on the left of the church are the farms and the mill on the way to Oakley and Crowell.

High Street and West Down, Chinnor, in 1910. This view has greatly changed with the addition of a shopping parade and new post office.

High Street, seen here in 1910, still has a number of eighteenth-century brick and flint houses of all sizes.

Station Road, Chinnor, looking east towards the Chilterns. The Black Boy has now been replaced with a later version, and the thatched cottages in the foreground have gone. This was Duck Square, where a little cottage industry was carried on, farming and packing ducks to send to the London markets.

Wycombe Road, Chinnor, c. 1910, leading east towards the Chilterns on the skyline. The Crown pub on the left must have been a welcome sight.

Lower Road, Chinnor.

Bledlow Road and the Lower Icknield Way, looking in the direction of Princes Risborough. Mr Ling's drapery is the white shop, with the Unicorn pub beyond (now a private house). The Red Lion is on the opposite corner. Doveleat and Elderdene housing estates, named after the houses that were pulled down, have been built in the orchards that back on to both sides of the road.

Chinnor had a pub on every corner. This one is the Red Lion at the Lower Road end of the High Street, looking towards the Chilterns. The double-fronted house in the centre is Doveleat, now surviving only in the name of the small estate of modern houses built in its garden and orchard.

Another corner pub in Chinnor is the Bird in Hand on Station Road, with Laburnham Cottage opposite (still thatched here in 1910).

Forge Cottage on Station Road, Chinnor, in the 1960s, with its bricks and flints whitewashed.

Forge Cottage and the Old Forge, Station Road, 1971. The Old Forge, empty for years, is being turned into a craft shop with some DIY shelving and lots of white paint. Photographer Leslie Wesson lived in Forge Cottage and recorded the conversion with interest.

Two views of Forge Crafts, open for business by autumn 1971. It was the only shop in Chinnor not selling everyday essentials.

W.H. Siarey and Son's timber yard in 1961. Chinnor had over forty chairmakers in the mid-nineteenth century; a survival is Chairmakers on the High Street. This cottage industry declined with the mechanization of furniture-making at High Wycombe and with the importation of foreign timber, but the managed Chiltern woodlands still provide work locally.

The early beehive kilns in the 1920s. Chinnor is known by its cement works which can be seen from miles away, even from the M40. They are a comparatively recent addition to the village, having been set up in 1908.

Chamber kilns in the 1920s. There is much to interest the industrial archaeologist in the Chinnor cement works.

A section of the Watlington branch line served the cement works, and the supply of fuel and raw materials kept the line open to Chinnor after it had closed elsewhere. Passenger traffic was stopped in 1957, other freight in 1961. The works were modernized in the 1950s and are seen here in 1973.

A view of Chinnor's cement works in the 1950s.

Above the spring-line villages loom the Chilterns, which are now almost entirely composed of beech trees managed for timber. Formerly chair-bodgers worked among the woods during the winter in temporary huts, and villagers regularly collected brush or coppice wood for fuel, and ash and oak for implements.

A view over Ewelme from the church tower, showing the school allotments across to Burrows Hill, where Chaucer Cottage, Burrows Hill Cottage and Aquelia lead down to the main street to the beckoning Greyhound Inn, with its five-bay frontage and two dormer windows. The Greyhound is now a private house. The Manor, seen in the distance, was the seat of the Chaucers, and then the de la Poles when Alice Chaucer married the Earl of Suffolk. It was known as 'The Palace' because it was used by Henry VIII and Elizabeth I as a country residence. After this it fell into ruins, and the Georgian manor house seen here was built from the remains.

A view of Ewelme from the downs to the west. The magnificent barns of Ford's Farm are in the right foreground, with the school situated just below the church.

The almshouses, Ewelme. Built like a miniature college quadrangle, with wooden cloister and carved arched doorways and bargeboards, the building forms part of the peaceful ensemble of charitable foundations of William and Alice de la Pole, Duke and Duchess of Suffolk, who held the manor in the fifteenth century. The thirteen almsmen wore cloaks with red crosses.

The fifteenth-century brick doorway to the almshouses, a creative use of brick imitating stone.

View from the top of Burrows Hill, Ewelme, with Chaucer Cottage on the right, and the churchyard and school allotments on the left.

Amy Stevens, later Reeves, stands outside The Shepherd's Hut in the 1930s. The pub was situated at the lower end of Ewelme, opposite a major watercress bed. Amy took over the pub from her parents and ran it with her husband until the 1980s. Beyond is the former bakery, looking up the village street towards the church.

Dormer Villa, or Cottage, with visitors (possibly Sydney Winfield and his wife in the milk cart). This view up the street has hardly changed except for the disappearance of the railings.

Ewelme High Street, *c.* 1895, photographed by Henry Taunt of Oxford. One of the little girls was possibly Daisy Winfield.

High Street, with the Greyhound (now a private house) on the left.

Lower End, Ewelme, on the way to Benson. Only the house on the left survives.

Poupart's Stores on Burrows Hill, *c.* 1910.

King's Pool was formed by the spring which feeds the nearly mile-long watercress brook along the village high street. Watercress was a cash crop here from the late nineteenth century for nearly a hundred years. It still grows wild.

The water cart crossing King's Pool, another Taunt scene.

The watercress harvest recorded by Taunt. This photograph shows a wonderful collection of wicker baskets, barrows and harvesting tools, and the working gear – boots, hats, vests and trousers tied up with string. The cottage on the left has been demolished; Brownings is the house on the right.

Gathering watercress at Ewelme, 1930–40. This was done in the spring, after the winter thaw and rains and before any summer drought. There were usually two crops, with another one in the autumn.

Representing watercress. Ewelme won first prize in this competition in Oxford, with an entry that does nothing to dispel the country bumpkin stereotype of farming folk.

Inside Chalkin's Stores, formerly Poupart's, and now a private house on Burrows Hill in Ewelme. The shop was a pottery studio in the late 1970s and early 1980s, which gave it its current name of Old Pottery.

Great Haseley manor house and church, 1904. The seventeenth-century manor house has three attractive dormer windows and projecting side wings which are not symmetrical. There is a tithe barn near the church, which dates from around 1400.

Great Haseley village, *c.* 1910.

Great Haseley village shop and street in the 1920s. The village lies near to limestone quarries around Little Milton, and has a number of stone buildings.

Gateway to the manor house, Great Milton, *c.* 1900. The manor house is a fifteenth-century building, altered and extended in the sixteenth and seventeenth centuries, but preserving some of its late medieval arrangement inside. This baroque gateway dates from the seventeenth-century enlargement. Another entrance leads to the manor house, now the restaurant Manoir au Quat' Saisons.

A view from the hill, Great Milton, *c.* 1870. In 1813 Arthur Young wrote in his report to the Board of Agriculture: 'Milton Field is one of the finest soils I have met with in the county: a dry, sound, friable loam or gravel convertible land, as they call it in Oxfordshire; but I know not why, unless that it is generally good for everything.'

Great Milton Priory. The Priory has both sixteenth- and seventeenth-century wings, with the arms of the Boyle family over the doorway. The village has several large houses.

The High Street, Great Milton.

The Green, Great Milton, *c.* 1911. A long row of seventeenth- and eighteenth-century stone cottages lines the triangular green.

Some of the handsome stone houses in Great Milton in 1907.

The neat village street in the 1930s.

The village, Great Milton, *c*. 1910. The prosperity of the Miltons contrasts with the poverty of those in the vale around Thame. The stone quarries here provided another trade, and the fields were more productive.

Great Milton, *c*. 1900. Villagers turn out on to The Green for a postcard portrait.

Great Milton village, 1910.

Haseley Road, Little Milton, *c.* 1910.

Old Toll House Corner, Stadhampton, on the Oxford–Watlington turnpike road.

Stadhampton is a large village, with an equally large green, which still celebrates its yearly village feast.

The village street and the Black Horse, Stadhampton, in 1939.

Chiselhampton Bridge, near Stadhampton, in 1904. This arched bridge made of Headington stone dates from the fifteenth to sixteenth century, which means that inevitably it became a target in the local skirmishes at Chalgrove during the Civil War.

SECTION FOUR
Small Places

The Bank, Kingston Blount. A tiny village situated today at the foot of the Chiltern scarp, but in the nineteenth century it was still an important droveway stop on the spring line. There were a number of pubs, a draper, grocer, wine merchant, smithy, corn merchant, butcher, baker, post office and school. The Watlington branch railway line had a halt here.

The Sun public house and the church, Sydenham. The church is Early English, with some Norman features inside, but was almost completely rebuilt in the restoration of 1856.

A row of cottages, Sydenham. The timber-framed, thatched one in the centre is really three cottages.

Some sturdy Sydenham cottages built using local materials, with thatch or tile roofs.

A family outside their cottage in the 1920s.

Handsome half-timbered houses in Church Lane, Brightwell-cum-Sotwell, photographed in 1975. Traditional building materials in the village are timber, cob and thatch, with some houses built of brick, flint and tile.

Brightwell Baldwin, *c.* 1910.

School House Corner, Drayton St Leonard, in the 1920s. This tiny village, with a population of 265 in 1900, still supported a National School with sixty pupils, a post office, a pub and a blacksmith.

Easington church in 1914. This simple church dates from the fourteenth century, but contains Norman stonework from a former church – a doorway and some zig-zag moulding. Some of the restoration work was ill-informed, however, as fourteenth-century stained glass and a window roundel have been set inside out.

The chapel, Russell's Water, early this century.

CUXHAM.

The village street, Cuxham, looking at Old Row and Middle Farm, *c.* 1900. This prosperous village had several mills and farms; its major landowner and lord of the manor was, and still is, Merton College.

Waterstock post office, *c.* 1909. The manor house was pulled down in 1956 and the servants' quarters and stables converted into a house. There are only around seventy people still living in the village.

Waterperry village in the 1930s. A loop of the Thame produces some of the richest meadows in the vale, with good common grazing; the field name Mill Field indicates that there was a windmill in the parish.

Waterperry. The village is a street of small cottages, a few houses and the manor. The church indicates a substantial settlement from the Saxon period, and it is likely that this cottage has an ancient timber framework.

Waterperry House in the 1930s. This rather severe eighteenth-century front wing was added to the manor house by Sir John Curson, and further remodelling was done after 1813 by the Henleys. It is largely known now as an horticultural college and garden centre with interesting gardens open to the public. The name comes from the Anglo-Saxon for 'pear orchard'.

SECTION FIVE

A40 to M40:
Road and Rail

Waiting for the train from Princes Risborough at the Chinnor halt, 1910.

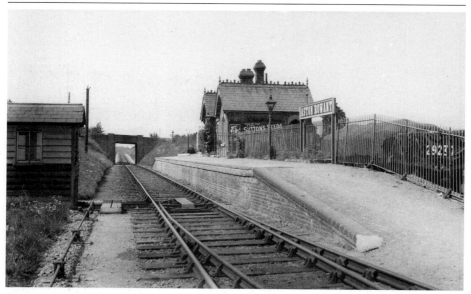

Aston Rowant railway station in 1919. This station on the Watlington branch line from Princes Risborough was used in films before its closure in 1957. It now serves as a storage depot.

Watlington station in its last week of operation. Some of the station buildings survived because of their use to the Shirburn Castle Estate for storing farm machinery. The track itself was taken up through Watlington parish as soon as the line closed.

The South Oxfordshire Hounds meet at the Three Pigeons, Tiddington, *c.* 1908.

The Toll House, Tetsworth, on the A40, photographed in 1985.

Swan Hill, Tetsworth, in 1907. The stables of the Swan Hotel on either side of the road once held over two hundred post and coach horses.

The Swan Hotel, Tetsworth, in the 1930s. The turnpiking of the Oxford to London road in 1718 made Tetsworth an important stopping place halfway between High Wycombe and Oxford. It was also on the crossroads of the 1773 turnpike from Thame to Wallingford, and carriers from all the surrounding villages met the Oxford and London-bound coaches there. The building itself, however, is older than the turnpikes – an inn has been here since the fourteenth century, and the present building is seventeenth century, remodelled with the chequerboard brickwork early in the eighteenth century. The centre wing served as the post office.

The Bungalow, Tetsworth, in the 1920s. The village went through a period of decline in the mid-nineteenth century when the turnpike traffic was diverted to the railways, but the motor car has reinstated the importance of the roads. This shop was probably very welcome on the long haul along the A40, but it was typical of the type of rural development deplored by those worried about the spoiling of the countryside for trippers.

Postcombe in the 1930s. The villages along the old turnpike road from London to Oxford find themselves at the mercy of fortune. First the turnpikes bring coach traffic, then the railways take it away; the motor car brings trippers to the country, the M40 takes them even further away.

The Feathers, Postcombe, in 1935. The village enjoyed modest development in the thirties without destructive levels of traffic.

Postcombe in the 1930s. Countryside activists even in the thirties deplored the ribbon development serving the needs of trippers to the countryside, but country bus services changed the lives of village people and enabled wider choices in work and holidays.

Lewknor High Street in the 1920s. The village was cut in two by this street, the main local road along the foot of the Chiltern scarp between Chinnor and Watlington, part of which is the Lower Icknield Way. The village school is on the left behind the trees.

The Crossways, Lewknor, *c.* 1920, looking towards the A40. Beyond the little post office, the road on the left leads to South Weston, and ahead is the Leathern Bottle pub, with the church and school in the distance.

The Nature Reserve, Aston Rowant, gives a good view looking south of the controversial cutting through the Chilterns made in 1972 for the M40. Lewknor's sheep walks lie either side of the road; the route of the A40 is on the northern side of Aston Hill, where the steep ascent and descent caused constant maintenance problems on the turnpike road.

Excavations along the route of the M40 from Stokenchurch to Waterstock were only a step ahead of the roadworks. Here the bulldozer clears the topsoil from the site of a Romano-British farmstead near Lewknor, while volunteers trowel away at pits and postholes. A new site was uncovered every few hundred metres, in spite of advance planning and active fieldwalking. Fifteen sites were eventually excavated, including Iron Age and Roman farmsteads, Roman and Saxon burial grounds, a medieval village and a woodland farmstead. The local press, which took this picture, were usually to hand in case of dramatic finds. The volunteer here is Nancy Stebbing, with Jonathan (age 1½) and Zoe (age 3), in May 1972.

The smithy, Sydenham, in the 1930s.

SECTION SIX
At Work

The old and the new – Joan and Nellie Bragginton pose as the tractor pulls a fully loaded Oxfordshire wagon on Manor Farm, Sydenham, and tows a hay rake, formerly drawn by horses. After the First World War the tractor began to have a mighty effect on the pace of change in the countryside. Instead of the whole village turning out for hay-making, for wages of three shillings a day, ten pence for women, a few hands could cut a field in a day.

The harvest at Sydenham in the 1920s. A large team of at least six horses is being used on this field. The man on the left carries a gun, perhaps for shooting rabbits.

A break in the fields, Sydenham, *c*. 1900.

Benjamin Rymills, cutting wood. A rare portrait of a farm labourer in his working clothes from Miss Deverell's collection from around Thame.

Farming with steam in 1938: Bill Tame with a traction engine at Brightwell-cum-Sotwell.

Harvey Castle at the cattle market, Thame. The countryman's smock survives alongside the contemporary 1920s gear of the ladies coming to market.

Alfred Burrows, saddler and harnessmaker, Great Milton, in 1910.

Watering place near Brownings, Ewelme. Until the Second World War all village cows were driven to common meadows and watered under the watch of the cowherd. Now the land is rented out by the Parish Council on behalf of the village.

Percy Seymore's village bakery, Chinnor, in 1961.

A shepherd leads his flock on the Towersey Road in the early part of this century, with a neat hay-rick in the background. This photograph also gives a good view of the open, flat landscape of the clay vale parishes.

A rest on the road from Chinnor to Thame, early this century.

The sheepwash, Sydenham, *c*. 1920.

Shearing time at Sydenham in the 1920s. Hand shears are being used although petrol or oil-powered tools were available.

A gamekeeper at Sydenham, *c.* 1900.

SECTION SEVEN
Wind and Watermills

Great Haseley windmill before restoration, showing the original door and window arrangement, now replaced with sashes, and the ogee finial cap.

Great Haseley windmill, derelict in the 1950s, is a tower mill which would have had two pairs of stones. It was built in 1760; an 1806 datestone probably refers to a substantial repair, and further repairs were made in 1889 by a local foundry. The mill was working until the early years of this century.

Great Haseley windmill under restoration in 1975.

The windmill at Little Milton was in decay by 1900; it lacked the handsome ogee-shaped cap which was common in this area.

Chinnor windmill, Mill Lane, *c.* 1895. This large wooden post-mill has a chequer-board, brick-built roundhouse and a ground level fantail (out of the picture, right). It dates from the eighteenth century and was working through to the 1920s. After having been sold, taken down and moved to the Essex-Suffolk area, it has now been brought back to Chinnor for restoration.

Great Milton windmill, *c.* 1900, around the time it went out of use. There were a number of windmills on this slight plateau in the Oxford vale – Great Haseley, Great and Little Milton were working up to 1900, this one was demolished in 1910. Others in the area are now known only through field names, as at Postcombe, Towersey, Lewknor, Albury, Sydenham, Thame, Waterperry and Waterstock.

The mill on the Crowell brook, Sydenham.

A group, including some millworkers, outside Sydenham mill, *c.* 1910.

Waterstock mill in the 1930s. This mill on the River Thame dates from Elizabethan times, and the tiny village has a single street of rubblestone and timber-framed houses.

The mill at Chalgrove. The large village mill gives an idea of the productivity of these vale village fields, and the power of the tiny village brooks. Margaret Lawrence (née Nixey), who is the girl in the photograph, still lives there. The old sheepwash is in the foreground.

SECTION EIGHT
Some Traditional Buildings

The Bird Cage Inn on Cornmarket, Thame, in the 1920s. This fifteenth-century inn has now been restored to display its original timbered structure, fortunately preserved under the dreadful rendering. It is a gem, with its jettied stories, window details and decorative timberwork. Inside are original fireplaces and a stone-vaulted cellar.

The Green at Chalgrove in a carefully composed postcard photograph of around 1900.

Tudor Cottages on the High Street, Chalgrove, 1904.

Shirburn Castle, near Watlington, in 1905. The castle, built shortly after 1377, is the earliest brick building in the county and occupies the site of an earlier moated manor house. In 1716 the Earl of Macclesfield bought it and made a number of alterations.

The thatcher at work on an eighteenth-century Sydenham cottage known as 'Thatchings' in the 1960s.

Cottage housing at Sydenham. A mixture of building materials is used in this cottage, which has been added to over and over: cob and thatch, then half-timbering, and brick and flint, under a tiled roof.

Smockacre, in Ewelme High Street, is a very old double cottage (seen here at the turn of the century).

The crossroads at King's Pool, Ewelme, with the village club in the background (now known as the Reading Room). After much debate it is currently being re-thatched.

Abbot's House at Brightwell-cum-Sotwell in 1979. The village has a number of handsome houses dating from the 1500s.

A wall painting photographed inside Abbot's House in 1931.

Longthatch on the Lower Icknield Way, Chinnor, in 1970. This part seventeenth-century cottage was one of the few which escaped the Royalist burning of much of the village during the Civil War. The right hand side, which is seventeenth century, has cob walls; the left, added later, is of brick and some flint, with inglenook fireplaces at each end and a bread oven. The original windows have since been replaced with modern versions.

A derelict cottage at Chinnor in 1972, side by side with modern infill in 1972. The village was allowed to develop rapidly in the 1960s; its population has grown to six times its 1901 census figure of 1,002.

The Chairmaker's Arms (left) on Chinnor High Street is a good example of the way publicans often combined two trades for a living. Unfortunately the thatched barn next to it burned down.

Great Haseley village expanded in the 1700s with a number of stone and thatch cottage rows (Long Row cost £173 to build). However, in 1885 a fire started by a spark from the laundry falling onto a thatched roof caused the destruction of six cottages because the fire appliance had to be summoned from Thame.

Thame Park in September 1904. The estate was built on the remains of the Cistercian Abbey of Thame, which was dissolved in the 1530s, and came into the possession of Lord Williams. He left it to one of his daughters, who married a Wenman. This view is of the sixteenth-century Abbot's lodgings, now a wing of the grand house built in the eighteenth century.

Oxford Road, Thame, in 1880. This yeoman farmhouse of around 1600 still looks down on the traffic from Oxford. It has the unusual feature of a double-storey bay window on the front. The farmhouse has since been greatly restored.

Prebendal House, Thame, west of the church. The moated complex of farm, hall, chapel and outbuildings served the administration of the Diocese of Lincoln and date from the thirteenth century. After being in a ruinous state the surviving buildings have been converted into a farm built around a courtyard. There are still many early features, although the moat has been filled in.

Prebendal House and chapel in 1910. The wall of the ruinous medieval hall lies between the chapel on the right and the solar wing, now restored to form the house, on the left. It was added to in the fourteenth and fifteenth centuries to make an impressive moated manor. The chapel is unaltered from the thirteenth century.

This cottage, known as Thatched House, on Chalgrove High Street has now gone.

Rose Cottage on Chalgrove High Street.

Places and Faces: Schools

The school at Brightwell-cum-Sotwell early in the century. The village school was moved to a new building in 1961 and the old school, with its clock tower, was restored and converted into a village hall in 1974/5.

A school group at Brightwell Baldwin in 1905.

A school outing by open charabanc from Brightwell-cum-Sotwell to Southsea in 1924.

Standard 2 class at Lewknor School in 1880.

A school group outside Sydenham School in the 1920s. The little Victorian (1849) school is built in the local brick and flint with cottagey windows. It closed in 1949 and is now the village hall.

A Victorian school interior at Chinnor in 1906. The National School was designed by G.E. Street and built in 1860 for £800.

Some self-conscious children eating school dinner at Chinnor in 1937.

Watlington School, the National School built in 1872, *c.* 1890.

Great Milton School, 1910. The sixteenth-century schoolhouse on the left has been sympathetically matched by the Victorian wing added in 1854.

The school at Ewelme. This stunning fifteenth-century schoolhouse was part of the foundation of the Duke and Duchess of Suffolk, William de la Pole and Alice, granddaughter of Geoffrey Chaucer. It was built of brick (probably bricks made at Nettlebed) in 1437 and, with the almshouses, is an early use of brick in the county. It is still a County Primary School.

View from Burrows Hill, Ewelme, towards the church, showing the almshouses and the tidy school allotments, *c.* 1960.

Class of *c.* 1902 outside Ewelme School gate. The student teacher is Minnie Harris, who lived in the village until she died in her eighties.

A school class, Ewelme, at the turn of the century; Mr Hermon was master between 1889 and 1926.

Old buildings at Lord Williams Grammar School, Thame, *c.* 1883. The endowment of 1559 provided a master's house (seen here, facing the road) and a schoolroom (behind). The house, with the arms of Lord Williams over the door, dates from 1569, with some repairs as a result of the Civil War, and additions in 1842. By 1883 the school itself had moved to new buildings on Oxford Road. The house is now used for offices.

New buildings at Lord Williams Grammar School, Thame, *c.* 1886. The school had to be re-founded after an inquiry of 1869 reported scandalous neglect of teaching duties and lack of discipline, so much so that there were only a few boys registered in the 1860s, and for a while the master had the school to himself. New College, which had supplied the masters, reformed the school and had these new buildings built between 1877 and 1879 by William Wilkinson. The style fits the Tudor origins of the foundation.

The hall at Lord Williams Grammar School, *c.* 1887.

School cricket, *c.* 1895.

Swimming lessons at the Church of England mixed school in the 1920s. The Anglican Church founded the National School in Thame in 1838, and this eventually became the Secondary Modern School in 1949, with new buildings in Hog Fair.

Gardening class for boys at the Church of England mixed school in the 1920s.

Domestic science class for girls at the Church of England mixed school in 1937.

Another domestic science class for girls at the Church of England mixed school in 1937.

Classroom at the Girls Grammar School, Thame, 1920s.

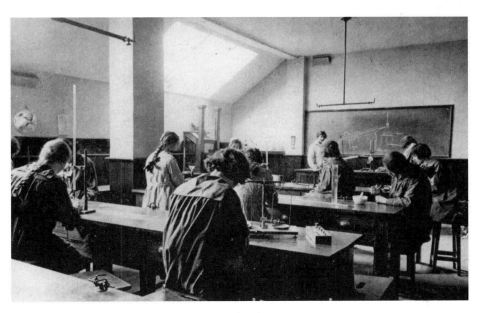

The Science Room at the Girls Grammar School, 1920s.

Swimming lessons at the Girls Grammar School, Thame, in the 1920s. The school took over the former Oxford County School building on the High Street, a large seventeenth-century house with a side entrance and buildings behind, which was remodelled in the eighteenth century. This handsome Georgian-fronted, six-bay, three-storeyed building was unfortunately demolished in 1965 to make way for a supermarket.

The gymnasium at the Girls Grammar School in the 1920s.

Serving the Community

The war memorial on The Green at Chalgrove. It is still well kept although details have changed, and the village often wins the 'Best-Kept' awards in its class.

Fire in the thatched cottage Smockacre on the High Street, Ewelme, in the 1980s. Fires were often caused by sparks from the chimney, but this one is thought to have been started by sparks from the overhead electricity wires in a high wind. The cottage was re-thatched.

Watlington Volunteer Fire Brigade outside the thatched barn.

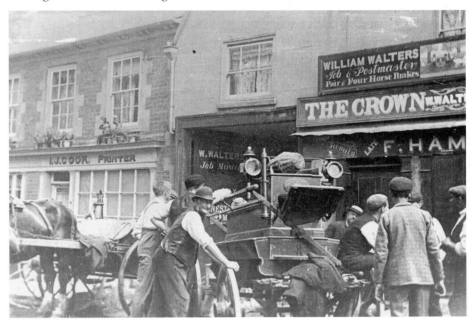

A lively scene in Watlington High Street in 1910, with the fire appliance outside The Crown. From The Crown the entrepreneurial William Walters operated a jobbing and horse brake business; he was also postmaster and publican. Cook, the printer next door, produced many of the postcards of Watlington. The shop is now the newsagent.

Carters Supply Store, Watlington, in 1905. The store, situated on the corner of High Street and Couching Street, suffered more than one fire. Note the Three Tuns pub sign; the pub is now an antiques shop.

Watlington Cottage Hospital, Hill Road. The building was erected in 1865 at the expense of the Earl of Macclesfield as a school for ten to twelve girls to learn domestic service.

The Home Guard, Ewelme, in the school playground. Back row, left to right: Tom Gemmell, Steve Beecham, Fane Orpwood, H.W. Jack Winfield Sr. Middle row: Mr Quixley, Charles Greenaway(?), Harry Scone, Vince Jackson. Front row: Sir Donald Somerville, Charles Cutler (baker), Mr Clark (gardener), Arthur Walden, Fred Harwood. Front: Sgt Theodore (Dorie) Winfield.

Scout parade, Watlington, probably on August Bank Holiday to raise money for the hospital. This one must have been after the 1907 restoration of the Town Hall. It is a summertime scene, with straw hats and lawn blouses.

Sydenham: portrait of a woman with a clay pipe, *c.* 1900.

Village Life and People

Villagers of Sydenham, *c*. 1900. Lacemaking was taught at a very early age in the villages along the Chiltern scarp; there were four lace schools at nearby Chinnor, where children worked eleven hours a day. Throughout the region the wives of agricultural labourers used this skill to supplement low wages. Lace feasts were held every fortnight, but the outworkers were firmly in the grip of the buyers who also supplied the patterns and the threads, which were imported from Holland. Most of the lace was bought by them for the London market.

Sydenham: a fiddler, *c*. 1920.

A family portrait at Sydenham, *c.* 1900.

A group poses outside the Four Horseshoes pub at Sydenham, *c.* 1900.

Sydenham: Club day, portrait of the band, *c.* 1900.

Portrait of the Sydenham villagers on Club day, *c.* 1900. The area around Thame suffered extreme poverty in the mid-nineteenth century and a number of families from Sydenham were helped to emigrate to Australia. Nine families with a total of thirty-two children left the village in 1843/4.

Club day at Sydenham, *c.* 1900.

The May Pole and flower show at Great Milton in 1907.

The Temperance Band, Chalgrove, *c.* 1906. There were two bands in the village, the Temperance and the Beershifters. Standing in the centre with the drum is Sam Belsen, the carrier, whose cart is in the background.

George V's Jubilee celebrations at Chalgrove. Few of these children are still in the village except the boy in the centre with the rosette and drum, Fred Woodward, and the fancy dress prize-winner, the girl on the left with the pram draped in the flag, now Mrs Godfrey.

The village feast, Chalgrove, in the 1920s. The Sunday before the feast was called Hospital Sunday, when a collection was made.

A group of farm workers, of all ages, from Dormers Leys, near Thame, from Miss Deverell's collection.

The estate employees at Thame Park in the early part of this century.

Group portrait of the men and boys at Brightwell-cum-Sotwell, *c.* 1910.

Rose Cottage, also known as Dolly Cottage, and Kings Cottage, Chalgrove, seen here with the brook in flood. Serious floods often arose from the innocent-looking brook; in 1879 twenty-two houses were flooded. The two cottages were demolished in the 1960s to make way for the senior citizens' bungalows on the High Street.

Moses Winfield, dairyman, and family of Ewelme. Left to right: Eva, Beatrice, Helen, Daisy, Edgar (who died in the Boer War), Sydney and Horace. This old Ewelme family name is said to come from Wingfield in Suffolk, from where the de la Poles brought builders and other servants for the church.

Members of the Ewelme Whist and Social Club, 1939–45. Back row, left to right: Mr Strickland, Albert Bryant, Mr Scone, Mr Millard, Winnie Justins, Dorothy Young, Mr Clark, Fred Harwood, -?- , Mr Young, Albert Munday. Middle row: -?-, Lizzie Winfield, Mrs Foster, Miss Coombs, Norah Harwood, Mrs Young, Mrs Strickland, Mrs King, Mrs Henry Shepherd, Miss Strickland, Mrs Albert Munday. Front row: -?-, Minnie Harris, Mrs Upton, Miss Doris Scaldwell, Mrs Brookes, Mrs May, Mrs Clark, Mrs Holland, Mrs Davies, Mrs Bond.

The General Stores, Ewelme, *c.* 1940, was known sometimes as Greenaway's after Fred Greenaway. It was in the International chain for a time until it closed in the 1970s.

The village Tea Bar, Ewelme, in 1939, possibly at a village fête held in a local garden. The owner has kindly adapted the thatched summer-house for the occasion.

Folk dancing with the morris men in Thame market place in the 1950s – perhaps a coronation celebration?

Acknowledgements

The author would like to thank the following individuals or institutions for the loan of photographs, or for help with information in compiling the text. Many of the photographs come from Oxfordshire County Council's photographic collection held by the Department of Leisure and Arts in the Centre for Oxfordshire Studies, Westgate, Oxford. Much additional detail, however, is collected by local history groups who take the time to interview long-standing residents of their village with the aim of recording memories and information which would otherwise be lost. I am grateful for their generosity in sharing their local knowledge and the results of their research.

Kath Baker • Peter Bradley • Hazel Carey • Judy Crockett, Watlington Parish History Group • Sian Ellis • Sue Etchells • Dr Malcolm Graham, Head of Oxfordshire Studies • Nuala La Vertu, Centre for Oxfordshire Studies
Kathy Lemaire, Ewelme Local History Society • *Oxford Mail*
Tony Rowse, Rowse Honey Ltd • Rural History Centre, University of Reading
John Steel-Clark, Chalgrove Local History Group
Leslie Wesson, Photographer